Warren Buffett
Hacked

Written by Matt Banks

'I always knew I was going to be rich. Never doubted it for a minute.' Warren Buffett.

Copyright © 2019 Matt Banks

ISBN-13: 978-0-6485687-1-1

ISBN-10: 0-6485687-1-7

www.hackedbooks.com

Introduction

Many investors and entrepreneurs try to be too smart or grow too big, only to end up accumulating more risk. Instead, Buffett keeps it simple by operating in areas of his competence while avoiding obvious mistakes like excessive debt and over-trading.

This Hacked book will show you the exact skills and personal traits Buffett needed to build his company Berkshire Hathaway into what it is today with staggering annual revenues of $250 Billion + USD per year.

I see Buffett's recipe to success boils down to his ability and willingness to do these 5 things very well.

1. He reads 5-6 hours per day
2. He rarely sells his stock
3. He is extremely patient
4. He is willing to miss new opportunities.
5. He avoids heavy debt

Through this book, we will touch on Buffett's methods and explain them in his own words.

Buffett has an obsession for simplicity and is happy to not be part of the next big thing. Avoiding unnecessary risks has made Buffett one of the richest men in the world today.

Within this book, you'll find Warren's most popular lessons arranged in a way that will have the most meaningful impact on your life.

Enjoy the book and remember you can continue the discussion online on hackedbooks.com and our social channels found on page 94.

About Hacked Books

Who do we write about?

The Hacked series of books are designed to take you into the minds of the captains of industries, the sports elite and other great thinkers throughout history.

Hacked series purpose

Our purpose is to make you the most focused and capable version of yourself. Our fast learning techniques use short form reading as a tool to get you there. Short form reading keeps you focused and propels your curiosity to find out more about the world.

Who is Hacked series for?

Hacked is for people who respect their time. We all know reading is the key to learning and insight into other worlds, however, reading a 300 + page book to get knowledge from the best minds is an inefficient way to obtain this information.

How do we do it, is this speed reading?

This is not simply 'Speed Reading;' it's better learning, by cutting out the worthless text and story loaded into books and articles. We specifically format and translate these lessons into short understandable blocks of text, so you can learn much faster.

'If you don't find a way to make money while you sleep, you will work until you die.'

Eyes on the prize.

Games are won by players who focus on the playing field — not by those whose eyes are glued to the scoreboard.

Just say no

You won't keep control of your time, unless you can say 'no.' You can't let other people set your agenda in life.

Investing in gold

Gold gets dug out of the ground in Africa, or someplace. Then we melt it down, dig another hole, bury it again and pay people to stand around guarding it. It has no utility. Anyone watching from Mars would be scratching their head.

Fool proofing

I try to invest in businesses that are so wonderful that an idiot can run them. Because sooner or later, one will.

Where is the risk?

When Charlie and I finish reading the long footnotes detailing the derivatives activities of major banks, the only thing we understand is that we don't understand how much risk the institution is running.

Change your methods

You know ... you keep doing the same things and you keep getting the same result over and over again.

On getting a job

Look for a job you would take if you didn't need a job.

Buffett on debt

I do not like debt and do not like to invest in companies that have too much debt, particularly long-term debt. With long-term debt, increases in interest rates can drastically affect company profits and make future cash flows less predictable.

Keep it simple

You're dealing with a lot of silly people in the marketplace; it's like a great big casino and everyone else is boozing. If you can stick with Pepsi, you should be O.K.

Buffett's long-term vision

I always knew I was going to be rich. I don't think I ever doubted it for a minute.

Bubble trouble

But a pin lies in wait for every bubble. And when the two eventually meet, a new wave of investors learns some very old lessons: First, many in Wall Street — a community in which quality control is not prized — will sell investors anything they will buy. Second, speculation is most dangerous when it looks easiest.

Keep reading

The more you learn, the more you earn.

Stop now

The most important thing to do if you find
yourself in a hole is to stop digging.

Remember it's still a horse

A horse that can count to ten is a remarkable
horse—not a remarkable mathematician.

'The Stock Market is designed to transfer money from the active to the patient.'

Life goals change over time

I do know that when I am 60, I should be attempting to achieve different personal goals than those which had priority at age 20.

Beware of geeks

Investors should be skeptical of history-based models. Constructed by a nerdy-sounding priesthood using esoteric terms such as beta, gamma, sigma and the like, these models tend to look impressive. Too often, though, investors forget to examine the assumptions behind the models. Beware of geeks bearing formulas.

Less is more

My life couldn't be happier. In fact, it'd be worse if I had six or eight houses. So, I have everything I need to have, and I don't need any more because it doesn't make a difference after a point.

Baby steps

I don't look to jump over 7-foot bars: I look around for 1-foot bars that I can step over.

Mindset

Unless you can watch your stock holding decline by 50% without becoming panic-stricken, you should not be in the stock market.

Plan for rain

Predicting rain doesn't count. Building arks does.

Thinking time

I insist on a lot of time being spent, almost every day, to just sit and think. That is very uncommon in American business. I read and think. So I do more reading and thinking, and make less impulse decisions than most people in business. I do it because I like this kind of life.

Buffett on reputation

It takes twenty years to build a reputation and five minutes to ruin it.

The Golden Rules

Rule No. 1 : Never lose money.

Rule No. 2 : Never forget Rule No. 1.

Actions have consequences

Never invest in a business you can't understand.

'The difference between successful people and very successful people is that very successful people say "no" to almost everything.'

True power

You will continue to suffer if you have an emotional reaction to everything that is said to you. True power is sitting back and observing things with magic. True power is restraint. If words control you that means everyone else can control you. Breathe and allow things to pass

Buffett on librarians.

If past history was all that is needed to play the game of money, the richest people would be librarians.

Master your craft

I knew a lot about what I did when I was 20. I had read a lot, and I aspired to learn everything I could about the subject.

Find value, buy low.

The critical investment factor is determining the intrinsic value of a business and paying a fair or bargain price.

Rich vs poor.

The rich invest in time, the poor invest in money.

Listen to yourself

People will always try to stop you from doing the right thing if it is unconventional.

Dangerous leverage

When you combine ignorance and leverage, you get some pretty interesting results.

'Honesty is a very expensive gift, don't expect it from cheap people.'

Value and market prices

Students need only two well-taught courses—
How to Value a Business, and How to Think
About Market Prices. Your goal as an investor
should simply be to purchase, at a rational price,
a part interest in an easily-understandable
business whose earnings are virtually certain to
be materially higher five, ten and twenty years
from now.

Over time, you will find only a few companies
that meet these standards—so when you see
one that qualifies, you should buy a meaningful
amount of stock.

You must also resist the temptation to stray
from your guidelines: If you aren't willing to own
a stock for ten years, don't even think about
owning it for ten minutes. Put together a
portfolio of companies whose aggregate
earnings march upward over the years, and so
also will the portfolio's market value. Though it's
seldom recognized, this is the exact approach.

Buying fancy things

If you buy things you do not need, soon you will have to sell things you don't need at a loss.

Polls lie

A public-opinion poll is no substitute for thought.

Avoid hysteria

A hyperactive stock market is the pickpocket of enterprise.

Buy and hold

An investor should ordinarily hold a small piece of an outstanding business with the same tenacity that an owner would exhibit if he owned all of that business.

'Risk comes from not knowing what you're doing.'

Less is more

You only have to do a very few things right in your life so long as you don't do too many things wrong.

When to be greedy

I will tell you the secret to getting rich on Wall Street. You try to be greedy when others are fearful. And you try to be fearful when others are greedy.

Plant your seeds today

Someone is sitting in the shade today because someone planted a tree a long time ago.

Good habits

The chains of habit are too light to be felt until they are too heavy to be broken.

Proceed with caution

A climate of fear is your friend when investing; a euphoric world is your enemy.

Cash and courage

Cash combined with courage in a time of crisis is priceless.

Life sorted

I really like my life. I've arranged my life so that I can do what I want.

Buy, don't rent

Buy a business, don't rent stocks.

If it's good, don't sell

We like to buy businesses, but we don't like to sell them.

Holding Vs Trading

I never attempt to make money on the stock market. I buy on the assumption that they could close the market the next day and not reopen it for five years.

Be a specialist

Risk can be greatly reduced by concentrating on only a few holdings.

A hidden tax

The arithmetic makes it plain that inflation is a far more devastating tax than anything that has been enacted by our legislature. The inflation tax has a fantastic ability to simply consume capital.

It makes no difference to a widow with her saving in a 5 percent passbook account whether she pays 100 percent income tax on her interest income during a period of zero inflation, or pays no income taxes during years of 5 percent inflation.

Either way, she is 'taxed' in a manner that leave her no real income whatsoever. Any money she spends comes right out of capital. She would find outrageous a 120 percent income tax, but doesn't seem to notice that 5 percent inflation is the economic equivalent.

Market bubbles

We will have another bubble, but usually you don't get it the same way you got it before.

Reading

When asked how he became so successful in investing, Buffett answered: *'We read hundreds and hundreds of annual reports every year.'*

Buffett on class war

There's class warfare, all right, but it's my class, the rich class, that's making war, and we're winning.

It's a waste of time

Stop trying to predict the direction of the stock market, the economy, interest rates, or elections.

'If you cannot control your emotions, you cannot control your money.'

Your entourage

It's better to hang out with people better than you. Pick out associates whose behavior is better than yours and you'll drift in that direction.

Always look back

In the business world, the rearview mirror is always clearer than the windshield.

Buy quality

Charlie and I would follow a buy-and-hold policy even if we ran a tax-exempt institution.

Inside or outside?

With enough insider information and a million dollars, you can go broke in a year.

Buyer beware

Stocks of companies selling commodity-like products should come with a warning label: "Competition may prove hazardous to human wealth."

Reading to riches

In fact, when Warren Buffett was once asked about the key to success, he pointed to a stack of nearby books and said, "Read 500 pages like this every day. That's how knowledge works. It builds up, like compound interest. All of you can do it, but I guarantee not many of you will do it.

When opportunity knocks

Opportunities come infrequently. When it rains gold, put out the bucket, not the thimble.

Focus on a niche

Diversification may preserve wealth, but concentration builds wealth.

Look for leaders

If you see somebody with even reasonable intelligence and a terrific passion for what they do and who can get people around them to march, even when those people can't see over the top of the next hill, things are going to happen.

HR Advice

In looking for people to hire, you look for three qualities: integrity, intelligence, and energy. And if they don't have the first, the other two will kill you.

Reading is key

Reading could be the BEST addiction one could have. The only proven side effect is imagination and an edge in knowledge.

Give back

If you're in the luckiest one per cent of humanity, you owe it to the rest of humanity to think about the other 99 per cent.

What's your advantage?

The key to investing is not assessing how much an industry is going to affect society, or how much it will grow, but rather determining the competitive advantage of any given company and, above all, the durability of that advantage.

How to save

Do not save what is left after spending; instead spend what is left after saving.

Buffett on buying Coca-Cola

I never buy anything unless I can fill out on a piece of paper my reasons. I may be wrong, but I would know the answer to that ...I'm paying $32 billion today for the Coca Cola Company because... If you can't answer that question, you shouldn't buy it. If you can answer that question, and you do it a few times, you'll make a lot of money

Look back

The best business returns are usually achieved by companies that are doing something quite similar today to what they were doing five or ten years ago.

What's your advantage?

The key to investing is not assessing how much an industry is going to affect society, or how much it will grow, but rather determining the competitive advantage of any given company and, above all, the durability of that advantage.

Keep to yourself

In some corner of the world they are probably still holding regular meetings of the Flat Earth Society. We derive no comfort because important people, vocal people, or great numbers of people agree with us. Nor do we derive comfort if they don't.

'Forecasts may tell you a great deal about the forecaster; they tell you nothing about the future.'

Why are you doing it?

You ought to be able to explain why you're taking the job you're taking, why you're making the investment you're making, or whatever it may be. And if it can't stand applying pencil to paper, you'd better think it through some more. And if you can't write an intelligent answer to those questions, don't do it.

Acquire useful knowledge

If you are investing in your education and you are learning, you should do that as early as you possibly can, because then it will have time to compound over the longest period. And that the things you do learn and invest in should be knowledge that is cumulative, so that the knowledge builds on itself. So instead of learning something that might become obsolete tomorrow, like some particular type of software [that no one even uses two years later], choose things that will make you smarter in 10 or 20 years.

Find a mentor

People always ask me where they should go to work, and I always tell them to go to work for whom they admire the most.

Be right, not busy

We don't get paid for activity, just for being right. As to how long we will wait, we'll wait indefinitely.

Intelligence isn't everything

You don't need to be a rocket scientist. Investing is not a game where the guy with the 160 IQ beats the guy with 130 IQ.

Your entourage

Tell me who your heroes are and I'll tell you how you'll turn out to be.

Market cycles

In the short term, the market is a popularity contest. In the long term, the market is a weighing machine.

Lack of change is good

Our approach is very much profiting from lack of change rather than from change. With Wrigley chewing gum, it's the lack of change that appeals to me.

Investing in startups

We make no attempt to pick the few winners that will emerge from an ocean of unproven enterprises. We're not smart enough to do that, and we know it. Instead, we try to apply Aesop's 2,600-year-old equation to opportunities in which we have reasonable confidence as to how many birds are in the bush and when they will emerge.

'The best thing that happens to us is when a great company gets into temporary trouble...We want to buy them when they're on the operating table.'

'AMEN'

We need a moderately-priced stock market...
The market, like the Lord, helps those who help
themselves. But, unlike the Lord, the market
does not forgive those who know not what they
do. For the investor, a too-high purchase price
for the stock of an excellent company can undo
the effects of a subsequent decade of favorable
business developments.

Derivatives

Derivatives are like sex. It's not who we're
sleeping with, it's who they're sleeping with
that's the problem.

Derivatives II

Derivatives are financial weapons of mass
destruction.

Be a specialist

What an investor needs is the ability to correctly evaluate selected businesses. Note that word "selected": you don't have to be an expert on every company, or even many. You only have to be able to evaluate companies within your circle of competence. The size of that circle is not very important; knowing its boundaries, however, is vital.

Warren on failing business's

Turnarounds seldom turn.

When to jump ship

Should you find yourself in a chronically leaking boat, energy devoted to changing vessels is likely to be more productive than energy devoted to patching leaks.

Love a discount

Long ago, Ben Graham taught me that 'Price is what you pay; value is what you get.' Whether we're talking about socks or stocks, I like buying quality merchandise when it is marked down.

Be passionate about what you do

Never give up searching for the job that you're passionate about. Try to find the job you'd have if you were independently rich. Forget about the pay. When you're associating with the people that you love, doing what you love, it doesn't get any better than that.

Don't fool yourself!

What the human being is best at doing is interpreting all new information so that their prior conclusions remain intact.

Get divorced

You need to divorce your mind from the crowd. The herd mentality causes all these IQ's to become paralyzed. I don't think investors are now acting more intelligently, despite the intelligence. Smart doesn't always equal rational. To be a successful investor you must divorce yourself from the fears and greed of the people around you, although it is almost impossible.

How to be right

You're neither right nor wrong because other people agree with you. You're right because your facts are right and your reasoning is right – that's the only thing that makes you right. And if your facts and reasoning are right, you don't have to worry about anybody else.

'Keep all your eggs in one basket but watch that basket closely.'

Be unpopular

Most people get interested in stocks when everyone else is. The time to get interested is when no one else is. You can't buy what is popular and do well.

Predictions are useless

A prediction about the direction of the stock market tells you nothing about where stocks are headed, but a whole lot about the person doing the predicting.

Wait for the perfect pitch

The stock market is a no-called-strike game. You don't have to swing at everything – you can wait for your perfect pitch.

Commodity investing

In a commodity business, it's very hard to be smarter than your dumbest competitor.

www.hackedbooks.com

Buffett's HR advice

Charlie and I believe our four criteria are essential if directors are to do their job — which, by law, is to faithfully represent owners. Yet these criteria are usually ignored. Instead, consultants and CEOs seeking board candidates will often say, "We're looking for a woman," or "a Hispanic," or "someone from abroad," or what have you. It sometimes sounds as if the mission is to stock Noah's ark. Over the years I've been queried many times about potential directors and have yet to hear anyone ask, "Does he think like an intelligent owner?"

Hedge your bets

Never depend on single income. Make investment to create a second source.

Put your money where your mouth is

Writing a check separates a commitment from a conversation

Hold on

All there is to investing is picking good stocks at good times and staying with them as long as they remain good companies.

Stay calm

The most important quality for an investor is temperament, not intellect. You need a temperament that neither derives great pleasure from being with the crowd or against the crowd.

Don't buy late

The investor of today does not profit from yesterday's growth.

Momentum is key

Life is like a snowball. The important thing is finding wet snow and a really long hill.

Keep it simple

It is not necessary to do extraordinary things to get extraordinary results.

Invest for value

For some reason, people take their cues from price action rather than from values. What doesn't work is when you start doing things that you don't understand or because they worked last week for somebody else. The dumbest reason in the world to buy a stock is because it's going up.

You need more than motivation

Without passion, you don't have energy. Without energy, you have nothing.

'A hyperactive stock market is the pickpocket of enterprise.'

Buy heritage

Buy companies with strong histories of profitability and with a dominant business franchise.

Prioritise sleep

I have pledged… to always run Berkshire with more than ample cash… I will not trade even a night's sleep for the chance of extra profits.

You get what you pay for

It's far better to buy a wonderful company at a fair price than a fair company at a wonderful price.

Purchase for the long term

Only buy something that you'd be perfectly happy to hold if the market shut down for 10 years.

Don't lose focus

Loss of focus is what most worries Charlie and me when we contemplate investing in businesses that in general look outstanding. All too often, we've seen value stagnate in the presence of hubris or of boredom that caused the attention of managers to wander.

Factors to Buffett's wealth

My wealth has come from a combination of living in America, some lucky genes, and compound interest.

How to get love

The only way to get love is to be lovable. It's very irritating if you have a lot of money. You'd like to think you could write a check: 'I'll buy a million dollars' worth of love.' But it doesn't work that way. The more you give love away, the more you get.

'Wall Street is the only place that people drive to in a Rolls Royce to take advice from people who ride the subway.'

Investment criteria

We select such investments on a long-term basis, weighing the same factors as would be involved in the purchase of 100% of an operating business:

(1) favorable long-term economic characteristics.

(2) competent and honest management.

(3) purchase price attractive when measured against the yardstick of value to a private owner.

(4) an industry with which we are familiar and whose long-term business characteristics we feel competent to judge.

Avoid big mistakes

An investor needs to do very few things right as long as he or she avoids big mistakes.

Don't stretch yourself

We will reject interesting opportunities rather than over-leverage our balance sheet.

Debt Vs Income

It's not debt per say that overwhelms an individual corporation or country. Rather it is a continuous increase of debt in relation to income that causes trouble.

Keep a level head

Nothing sedates rationality like large doses of effortless money.

Look for mistakes

Great investment opportunities come around when excellent companies are surrounded by unusual circumstances that cause the stock to be misappraised.

Know your limits

People who know the edge of their competency are safe, and those who don't, aren't.

Successful investing ingredients

Successful Investing takes time, discipline and patience. No matter how great the talent or effort, some things just take time.

Culture is King

Culture, more than rule books, determines how an organization behaves.

www.hackedbooks.com

'Never ask a barber if you need a haircut.'

When markets fall

So smile when you read a headline that says "Investors lose as market falls." Edit it in your mind to "Dis-investors lose as market falls—but investors gain." Though writers often forget this truism, there is a buyer for every seller and what hurts one necessarily helps the other. (As they say in golf matches: "Every putt makes someone happy.")

Warren on MBA's

Our experience with newly-minted MBAs has not been that great. Their academic records always look terrific and the candidates always know just what to say; but too often they are short on personal commitment to the company and general business savvy. It's difficult to teach a new dog old tricks.

Risk vs volatility

Volatility is not the same thing as risk, and anyone who thinks it is will cost themselves money.

Keep it real

I'm not interested in cars and my goal is not to make people envious. Don't confuse the cost of living with the standard of living.

Don't get caught in the rush

As we look at the major acquisitions that others made during 1982, our reaction is not envy, but relief that we were non-participants. For in many of these acquisitions, managerial intellect wilted in competition with managerial adrenaline. The thrill of the chase blinded the pursuers to the consequences of the catch.

'There is nothing wrong with a 'know nothing' investor who realizes it. The problem is when you are a 'know nothing' investor but you think you know something.'

How to spot a novice

If you've been playing poker for half an hour and you still don't know who the patsy is, you're the patsy.

How to live forever

Charlie's dictum: "All I want to know is where I'm going to die so I'll never go there."

Liquor and leverage

I've seen more people fail because of liquor and leverage — leverage being borrowed money. You really don't need leverage in this world much. If you're smart, you're going to make a lot of money without borrowing.

A blend of art and science

Valuing a business is part art and part science.

Managers over numbers

Accounting numbers, of course, are the language of business and as such are of enormous help to anyone evaluating the worth of a business and tracking its progress. Charlie and I would be lost without these numbers: they invariably are the starting point for us in evaluating our own businesses and those of others. Managers and owners need to remember, however, that accounting is but an aid to business thinking, never a substitute for it.

Diversification is ignorance

Diversification is a protection against ignorance. It makes very little sense for those who know what they're doing.

Stay focused

We don't have to be smarter than the rest; we have to be more disciplined than the rest.

Buffett on certainty

You know, people talk about this being an uncertain time. You know, all time is uncertain. I mean, it was uncertain back in – in 2007, we just didn't know it was uncertain. It was – uncertain on September 10th, 2001. It was uncertain on October 18th, 1987, you just didn't know it.

Do what you want

There comes a time when you ought to start doing what you want. Take a job that you love. You will jump out of bed in the morning. I think you are out of your mind if you keep taking jobs that you don't like because you think it will look good on your resume. Isn't that a little like saving up sex for your old age?

Invest in the USA

For 240 years, it's been a terrible mistake to bet against America.

'Diversification is protection against ignorance. It makes little sense if you know what you are doing.'

Stock forecasters

We've long felt that the only value of stock forecasters is to make fortune tellers look good. Even now, Charlie and I continue to believe that short-term market forecasts are poison and should be kept locked up in a safe place, away from children and also from grown-ups who behave in the market like children.

Low Prices

The most common cause of low prices is pessimism—sometimes pervasive, sometimes specific to a company or industry. We want to do business in such an environment, not because we like pessimism but because we like the prices it produces. It's optimism that is the enemy of the rational buyer.

Love vs greed

Not doing what we love in the name of greed is very poor management of our lives

How to pick a stock

Buy a stock the way you would buy a house.
Understand and like it such that you'd be
content to own it in the absence of any market

Dwarfs and giants

If each of us hires people who are smaller than
we are, we shall become a company of dwarfs.
But, if each of us hires people who are bigger
than we are, we shall become a company of
giants.

'As happens in Wall Street all too often, what the wise do in the beginning, fools do in the end.'

First-hand experience matters

By the age of 10, I'd read every book in the Omaha public library about investing, some twice. You need to fill your mind with various competing thoughts and decide which make sense. Then you have to jump in the water – take a small amount of money and do it yourself. Investing on paper is like reading a romance novel vs. doing something else. You'll soon find out whether you like it. The earlier you start, the better.

Good things take time

No matter how great the talent or efforts, some things just take time. You can't produce a baby in one month by getting nine women pregnant.

Price vs value

Price is what you pay. Value is what you get whether that value is good or bad value it's up to you.

Smart ducks don't quack

In a bull market, one must avoid the error of the preening duck that quacks boastfully after a torrential rainstorm, thinking that its paddling skills have caused it to rise in the world. A right-thinking duck would instead compare its position after the downpour to that of the other ducks on the pond.

Lose small

Anything can happen in stock markets and you ought to conduct your affairs so that if the most extraordinary events happen, that you're still around to play the next day.

Treasure quality people

Having first rate people on the team is more important than designing hierarchies and clarifying who reports to whom.

Buffett on reputation

When a management with a reputation for brilliance tackles a business with a reputation for bad economics, it is the reputation of the business that remains intact.

Choose carefully

An investor should act as though he had a lifetime decision card with just twenty punches on it.

What to look for

A great investment opportunity occurs when a marvelous business encounters a one-time huge, but solvable problem.

History lessons

What we learn from history is that people don't learn from history.

'I learned to go into business only with people whom I like, trust, and admire.'

Fear and gold

Gold is a way of going long on fear, and it has been a pretty good way of going long on fear from time to time. But you really have to hope people become more afraid in a year or two years than they are now. And if they become more afraid you make money, if they become less afraid you lose money, but the gold itself doesn't produce anything.

Think like an owner

For Buffett, managers are stewards of shareholder capital. The best managers think like owners in making business decisions.

When to buy

Only those who will be sellers of equities in the near future should be happy at seeing stocks rise. Prospective purchasers should much prefer sinking prices.

Buffett on inheritance

I believe in giving my kids enough so they can do anything, but not so much that they can do nothing.

Money and love

Money to some extent sometimes let you be in more interesting environments. But it can't change how many people love you or how healthy you are.

Patience is key

Time is the friend of the wonderful company, the enemy of the mediocre.

Simple over complex

Business schools reward complex behavior more than simple behavior, but simple behavior is more effective.

A life well lived

When you get to my age, you'll really measure your success in life by how many of the people you want to have love you actually do love you...If you get to my age in life and nobody thinks well of you, I don't care how big your bank account is, your life is a disaster. That's the ultimate test of how you have lived your life.

How to wipe debt

I could end the deficit in five minutes. You just pass a law that says that anytime there is a deficit of more than 3% of GDP all sitting members of congress are ineligible for reelection.

Why sell?

When we own portions of outstanding businesses with outstanding managements, our favorite holding period is forever.

'The most important investment you can make is in yourself.'

Perspective

Over the long term, the stock market news will be good. In the 20th century, the United States endured two world wars and other traumatic and expensive military conflicts; the Depression; a dozen or so recessions and financial panics; oil shocks; a fly epidemic; and the resignation of a disgraced president. Yet the Dow rose from 66 to 11,497.

Sad but true

There seems to be some perverse human characteristic that likes to make easy things difficult.

Buyer beware

A line from Bobby Bare's country song explains what too often happens with acquisitions: "I've never gone to bed with an ugly woman, but I've sure woke up with a few."

www.hackedbooks.com

Some opinions don't matter

In the 54 years Charlie Munger and I have worked together, we have never forgone an attractive purchase because of the macro or political environment, or the views of other people. In fact, these subjects never come up when we make decisions.

Do what you love

In the world of business, the people who are most successful are those who are doing what they love.

Wait for stability

Investors making purchases in an overheated market need to recognize that it may often take an extended period for the value of even an outstanding company to catch up with the price they paid.

Baseball investing

I call investing the greatest business in the world ... because you never have to swing. You stand at the plate, the pitcher throws you General Motors at 47! U.S. Steel at 39! and nobody calls a strike on you. There's no penalty except opportunity lost. All day you wait for the pitch you like; then when the fielders are asleep, you step up and hit it.

Buffett on folly

Look at market fluctuations as your friend rather than your enemy; profit from folly rather than participate in it.

When to act

You do things when the opportunities come along. I've had periods in my life when I've had a bundle of ideals come along, and I've had long dry spells. If I get an ideal next week, I'll do something. If not, I won't do a damn thing.

'Money is not everything. Make sure you earn a lot before speaking such nonsense.'

Interesting thoughts

But then it dawned on me that the opinion of someone who is always wrong has its own special utility to decision-makers.

The press is one-sided

Buffett once referred to a reporter in his speech: "He's not looking at quarterly earnings projections, he's not looking at next year's earnings, he's not thinking about what day of the week it is, he doesn't care what investment research from any place says, he's not interested in price momentum, volume or anything. He's simply asking: What is the business worth?"

Price well

Never count on making a good sale. Have the purchase price be so attractive that even a mediocre sale gives good results.

Self-belief

I had a great teacher in life in my father. But I had another great teacher of profession in terms of Ben Graham. I was lucky enough to get the right foundation very early on. And then basically I didn't listen to anybody else. I just look in the mirror every morning and the mirror always agrees with me. And I go out and do what I believe I should be doing. And I'm not influenced by what other people think.

Strong culture is King

Culture, more than rule books, determines how an organization behaves.

'The fact that people will be full of greed, fear, or folly is predictable. The sequence is not predictable.'

Wait for low tide

You never know who's swimming naked until the tide goes out.

Knowing when to enter and exit

The line separating investment and speculation, which is never bright and clear, becomes blurred still further when most market participants have recently enjoyed triumphs.

Nothing sedates rationality like large doses of effortless money. After a heady experience of that kind, normally sensible

people drift into behavior akin to that of Cinderella at the ball.

Continued from page 82

They know that overstaying the festivities —
that is, continuing to speculate in companies
that have gigantic valuations relative to the cash
they are likely to generate in the future — will
eventually bring on pumpkins and mice.

But they nevertheless hate to miss a single
minute of what is one helluva party. Therefore,
the giddy participants all plan to leave just
seconds before midnight. There's a problem,
though: They are dancing in a room in which the
clocks have no hands.

About Warren Buffett

Warren Edward Buffett was born August 30, 1930 in Omaha, Nebraska. He is an American business magnate, investor, speaker and philanthropist who is best known as the chairman and CEO of Berkshire Hathaway.

He is considered one of the most successful investors in the world with a current net worth of $89.9 billion USD as of May 4, 2019, making him the third-wealthiest person in the world.

Buffett developed an interest for business and investing in his youth, eventually entering the Wharton School of the University of Pennsylvania in 1947 before transferring and graduating from the University of Nebraska at the age of 19.

He then went on to graduate from Columbia Business School, where he molded his investment philosophy around the concept of value investing that was pioneered by Benjamin Graham.

After completing his Bachelors, Buffett attended New York Institute of Finance to focus his economics background and soon after began various business partnerships, including one with Graham.

He created Buffett Partnership, Ltd in 1956 and his firm eventually acquired a textile manufacturing firm called Berkshire Hathaway and assumed its name to create a diversified holding company.

Beside his business achievements, Buffett is a notable philanthropist, having pledged to give away 99 percent of his fortune to philanthropic causes.

What has Buffett invested in?

A current list of Warren Buffett's and Berkshire Hathaway's owned companies and investments.

APPLE INC

www.apple.com

BANK AMER CORP

www.bankofamerica.com

WELLS FARGO & CO NEW

www.wellsfargo.com

COCA COLA CO

www.coca-cola.com

AMERICAN EXPRESS CO

www.americanexpress.com

KRAFT HEINZ CO

www.kraftheinzcompany.com

US BANCORP DEL

www.usbank.com

JPMORGAN CHASE & CO

www.jpmorganchase.com

MOODYS CORP

www.moodys.com

BANK OF NEWYOR MELLON CORP

www.bnymellon.com

DELTA AIR LINES INC DEL

www.delta.com

GOLDMAN SACHS GROUP INC

www.goldmansachs.com

SOUTHWEST AIRLS CO

www.southwest.com

GENERAL MTRS CO

www.gm.com

VERISIGN INC

www.verisign.com

DAVITA HEALTHCARE PARTNERS

www.davitamedicalgroup.com

CHARTER COMMUNICATIONS INC

www.spectrum.com

UNITED CONTL HLDGS INC

U S G CORP

www.usg.com

VISA INC

www.visa.com

AMERICAN AIRLS GROUP INC

www.aa.com

LIBERTY MEDIA CORP DELAWARE

www.libertymedia.com

MASTERCARD INC

www.mastercard.us

PNC FINL SVCS GROUP INC

www.pnc.com

COSTCO WHSL CORP NEW

www.costco.com

RED HAT INC

www.redhat.com

AMAZON COM INC

www.amazon.com

M & T BK CORP

www.mtb.com

TRAVELERS COMPANIES INC

www.travelers.com

SIRIUS XM HLDGS INC

www.siriusxm.com

TEVA PHARMACEUTICAL INDS LTD

www.tevapharm.com

SYNCHRONY FINL

www.synchrony.com

STORE CAP CORP

www.storecapital.com

AXALTA COATING SYS LTD

www.axalta.com

STONECO LTD

www.stone.co

RESTAURANT BRANDS INTL INC

www.rbi.com

PHILLIPS 66

www.phillips66.com

TORCHMARK CORP

www.torchmarkcorp.com

LIBERTY GLOBAL PLC

www.libertyglobal.com

SUNCOR ENERGY INC

www.suncor.com

LIBERTY LATIN AMERICA LTD

www.lla.com

JOHNSON & JOHNSON

www.jnj.com

PROCTER & GAMBLE CO

www.pg.com

UNITED PARCEL SERVICE INC

www.ups.com

MONDELEZ INTL INC

www.mondelezinternational.com

To see our other book titles

See back of book or visit

www.hackedbooks.com

HACKED. PUBLISHERS

Join us online to follow the discussions

@hackdbookco

facebook.

@hackedbooks

Instagram

@BooksHacked

twitter

Dedication

This book is dedicated to you.

You have so much potential.

You are by no means only what you already know.

You are also all that which you could know, if you only would.

Thus, you should never sacrifice what you could be for what you are.

You should never give up the better that resides within for the security you already have—and certainly not when you have already caught a glimpse, an undeniable glimpse, of something beyond.

Richard Branson

HACKED

«DON'T JUST PLAY THE GAME –
– CHANGE IT FOR GOOD.»

Jeff Bezos

HACKED

«YOUR MARGIN IS MY OPPORTUNITY»

More Great Titles in the Hacked Series Coming Soon...

www.ingramcontent.com/pod-product-compliance
Lightning Source LLC
Chambersburg PA
CBHW020511030426
42337CB00011B/342